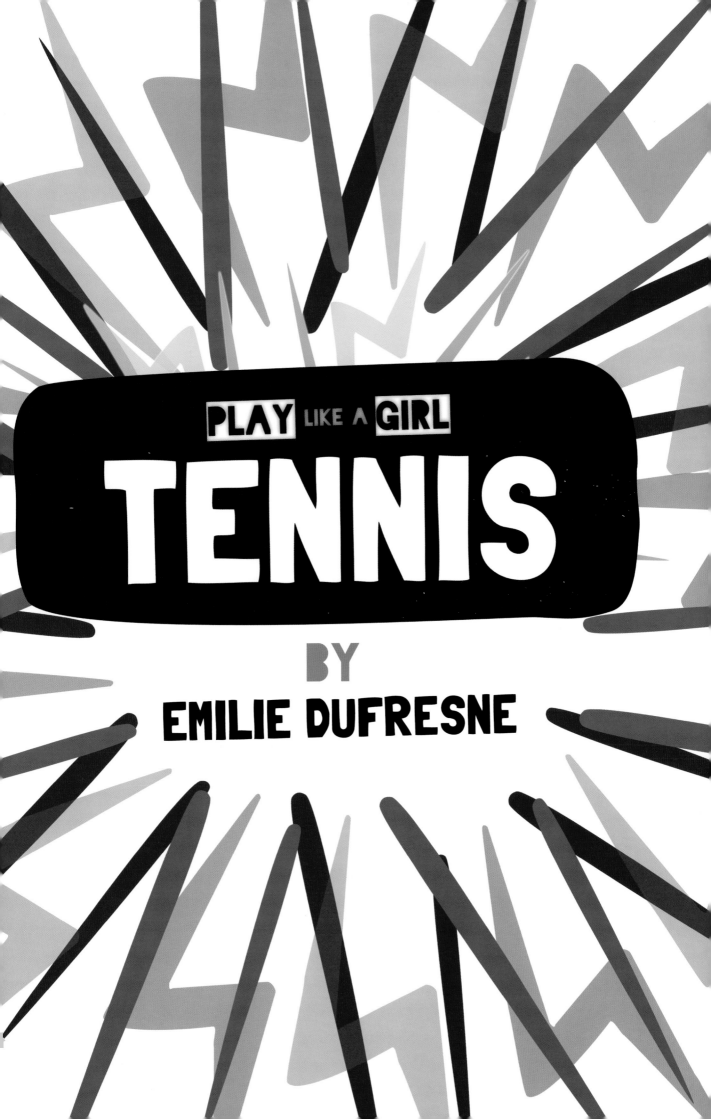

PLAY LIKE A GIRL

TENNIS

BY

EMILIE DUFRESNE

BookLife
PUBLISHING

©2019
BookLife Publishing Ltd.
King's Lynn
Norfolk PE30 4LS

ISBN: 978-1-78637-783-8

Written by:
Emilie Dufresne

Edited by:
Madeline Tyler

Designed by:
Danielle Jones

All rights reserved
Printed in Malaysia

A catalogue record for this book
is available from the British Library

All facts, statistics, web addresses and URLs
in this book were verified as valid and accurate
at time of writing. No responsibility for any
changes to external websites or references can
be accepted by either the author or publisher.

IMAGE CREDITS

CONTENTS

Words that look like <u>this</u> are tennis lingo. Learn more about them on page **8**.

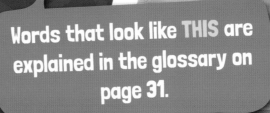

Words that look like **THIS** are explained in the glossary on page **31**.

THE BASICS
PEP TALK

So, you want to play tennis? This book will teach you all about what to say, what to wear and how to play. From learning the lingo to earning a place in the hall of fame, this book will give you the know-how!

GRAB YOUR FRIENDS AND RACKET – IT'S TIME TO PLAY!

RACKET

Tennis is a game that is played on a court. Depending on what type of tennis is being played, one or two people will play either side of the net. They use rackets to hit a tennis ball over the net. Players try and score points by hitting the ball so that their opponent cannot hit it back, but so that it bounces within the court lines.

TENNIS BALLS

Tennis is a game that requires a lot of skill and fitness. Players have to practise different types of moves and strokes. Tennis is also a very strategic sport. A bit like chess, players can plan a few moves ahead to try and gain the upper hand on their opponent.

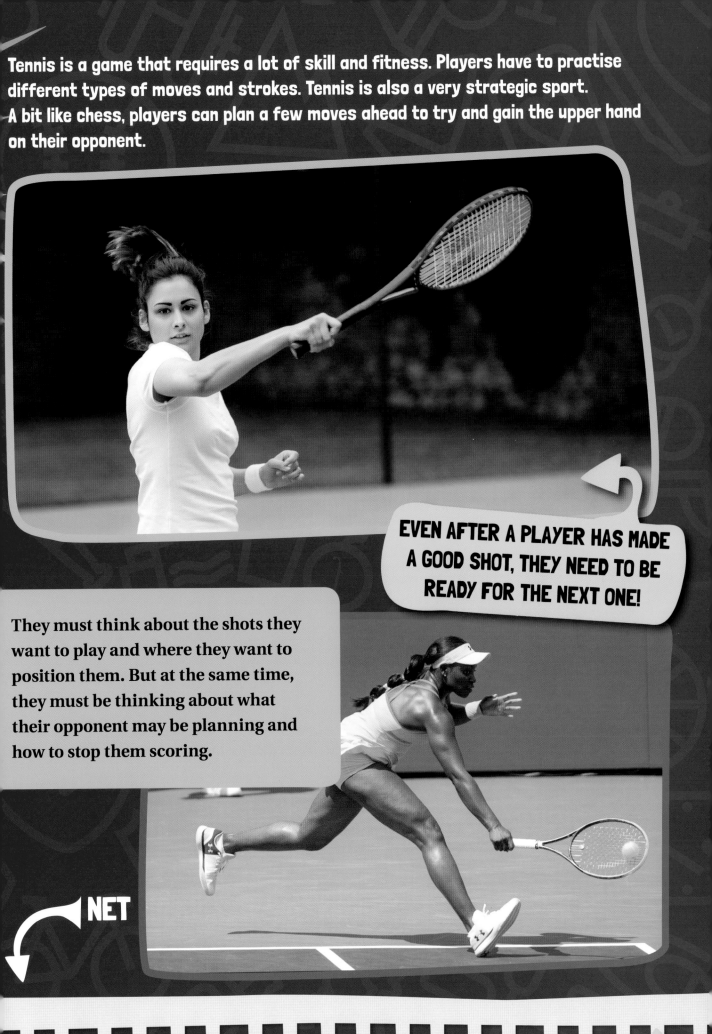

EVEN AFTER A PLAYER HAS MADE A GOOD SHOT, THEY NEED TO BE READY FOR THE NEXT ONE!

They must think about the shots they want to play and where they want to position them. But at the same time, they must be thinking about what their opponent may be planning and how to stop them scoring.

NET

THE TYPES

DOUBLES

Doubles tennis is a variation of tennis where two people play on one side of the court instead of just one person. Doubles teams can be made up of two players of the same sex; this could be two women playing against two women, or two men against two men. You can also play as mixed doubles, where a woman and a man play against a woman and a man.

MIXED DOUBLES

TABLE TENNIS

LIGHTWEIGHT BALL

BAT

TABLE

Also known as ping pong, this game is similar to tennis but on a smaller scale. Players hit a very lightweight ball using a rubber-coated racket or paddle. They have to hit the ball so that it bounces onto the table but try and make it hard for their opponent to hit the ball back.

TIBHAR S

6

WHEELCHAIR TENNIS

Wheelchair tennis is an adaptation of tennis for people who have disabilities in their legs. The variation is the same as the normal game, except the players use a wheelchair to MANOEUVRE around the court. The ball is also allowed to bounce twice before it has to be hit back.

DOUBLES WHEELCHAIR TENNIS MATCH

REAL TENNIS

Real tennis is the original game that developed into what we now call tennis. It is also known as royal tennis because many members of royalty used to play this game. Instead of the court being marked on the ground, real tennis courts have walls on either side. The ball is allowed to hit the walls and players score extra points if they manage to hit it into the gallery.

GALLERY

WALLED COURT

THE LINGO

The lingo, the slang, the vocab. Whatever you call it, learning the words behind specific sports can be a very daunting task! Here are some of the strangest and weirdest words that will help you talk the tennis talk in no time.

OFFENSIVELY
To play in a way that is actively trying to score points.

IN
When the ball lands within or touching the court BOUNDARIES, it is considered in.

SLICE
A type of tennis skill where a player hits the ball in such a way that it creates backspin on the ball and makes it hard for your opponent to reach (see page 13 for more information on slices).

ACE
A type of serve that is so hard or fast that the opponent doesn't even manage to hit it with their racket.

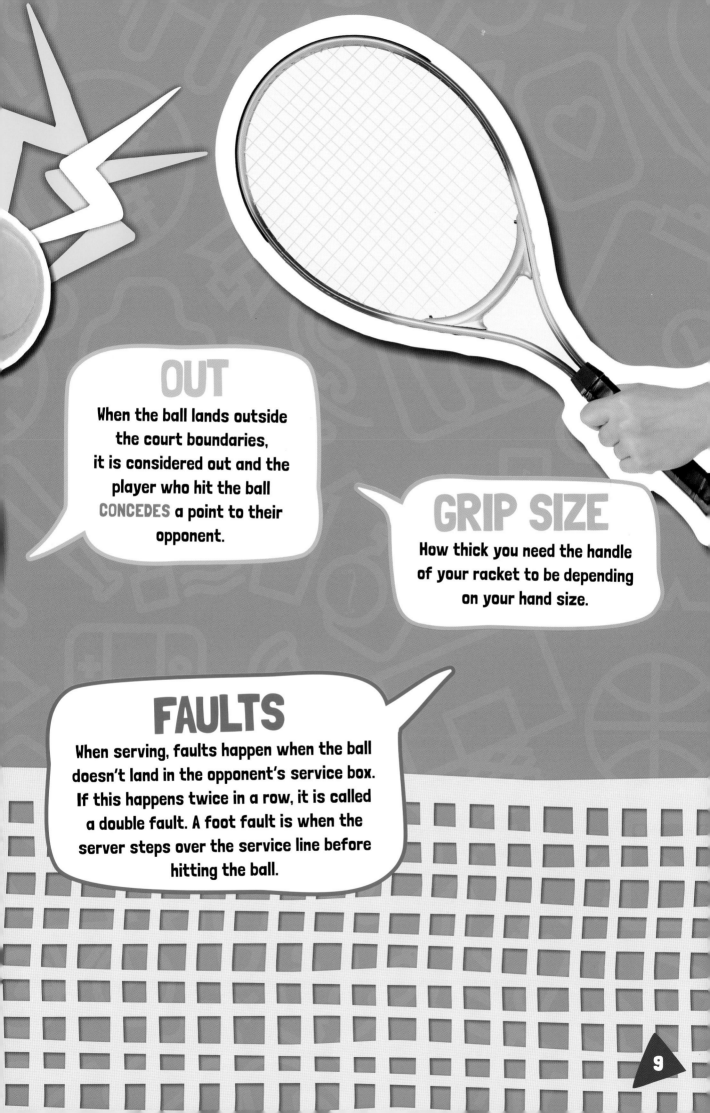

OUT

When the ball lands outside the court boundaries, it is considered out and the player who hit the ball CONCEDES a point to their opponent.

GRIP SIZE

How thick you need the handle of your racket to be depending on your hand size.

FAULTS

When serving, faults happen when the ball doesn't land in the opponent's service box. If this happens twice in a row, it is called a double fault. A foot fault is when the server steps over the service line before hitting the ball.

THE SKILLS

SERVES

Each point played begins with a serve. The player stands behind the baseline, throws the ball into the air and hits it. The player must hit the ball diagonally across the court so it lands in the box diagonally opposite where the server is standing.

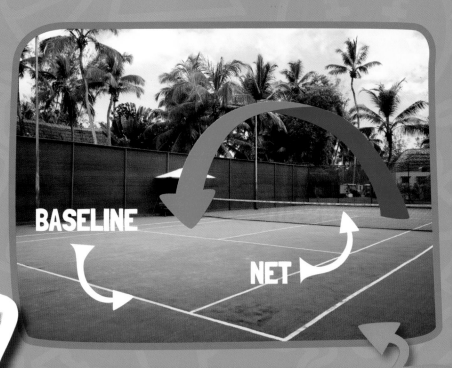

BASELINE

NET

IF THE BALL GOES INTO THE NET, OR DOESN'T LAND IN THE RIGHT PART OF THE COURT, THEN THE PLAYER GETS ANOTHER CHANCE TO SERVE. IF THE ERROR HAPPENS AGAIN, A POINT IS AWARDED TO THEIR OPPONEN

ACES

If you keep practising your serve then you might serve an <u>ace</u> during a game. This isn't a skill that can be taught, but if you keep practising then it is more likely to happen. An ace is when your serve is so fast, or so difficult to reach, that your opponent doesn't even get a chance to touch it with their racket. This means that the point is awarded to you instantly.

FIND OUT MORE ABOUT TENNIS SCORING ON PAGE 20.

FOREHAND

For a forehand shot, you hold the racket with your DOMINANT hand – this could be your right hand or your left hand. When hitting a forehand shot, stand facing the court with your racket straight out in front of you, swing your racket arm back and round, hitting the ball and following through by bringing your arm around your body.

BACKHAND

The backhand is the opposite to the forehand as you swing from the non-dominant side of your body. Begin by standing as you would for a forehand. When you can tell that the ball is travelling towards your non-dominant side, step backwards and bring the racket backwards. Swing it round your body and follow through.

THERE ARE ALSO SOME TYPES OF HIT THAT CAN HELP YOU SCORE POINTS BY PLAYING AND MOVING TACTICALLY.

VOLLEY

A volley is when a player hits the tennis ball before it has bounced on the ground. A player will usually have to make a volley shot if they have come closer to the net. This is often a tactical move that allows players to play <u>offensively</u> and hit the ball in a way that is very hard to hit back.

DROP SHOT

A drop shot is usually played when a player is standing close to the net. They hit the ball lightly so that it doesn't travel very far over the net. This makes it very hard for the opponent to run up to the net to hit the ball back.

> DEPENDING ON THE ANGLE AT WHICH YOUR RACKET PUSHES THE BALL, YOU CAN CREATE TOPSPIN AND BACKSPIN. THIS WILL CHANGE HOW THE BALL BOUNCES AND MOVES THROUGH THE AIR.

TOPSPIN

Hitting a ball with topspin makes the ball fall quicker than your opponent will expect. To give your shot some topspin, sweep your racket over the top of the ball as you swing. This makes the ball spin forwards as it travels through the air.

BACKSPIN

Hitting a ball with backspin makes the ball travel farther and bounce higher. To give your shot backspin, brush your racket underneath the ball as you hit it. This type of hit can also be called a <u>slice</u>. This makes the ball spin backwards as it is moving through the air.

THE KIT

Tennis is a very fast-paced sport that is a very good form of exercise. It works both your CARDIOVASCULAR SYSTEM and your muscles. Players are constantly running, swinging and jumping.

ALL OF THIS EXERCISE NEEDS THE RIGHT TYPE OF KIT!

A tennis player's kit usually consists of a top or t-shirt made of BREATHABLE fabric. This can be tight or baggy depending on your preferences. On the bottom, players can either wear shorts or a skirt. Some tennis players wear dresses. As long as you can move around easily and you are comfortable, you are ready to play tennis!

VISOR

SKIRT

TOP

SWEAT BAND

PLAYERS CAN ALSO WEAR SWEAT BANDS OR VISORS IF THEY WANT TO.

SHOES

Tennis can be played on four different types of court: grass, clay, hard and carpet. This means that there are four different types of shoe that are better suited to each different type of court. It is especially important for PROFESSIONAL tennis players to have the right type of trainer.

FOR EXAMPLE, ON GRASS COURTS YOU NEED TO HAVE SHOES WITH VERY GOOD GRIP SO THAT YOU DON'T SLIP OVER.

WIMBLEDON

Certain tournaments require their tennis players to wear certain types of outfit. For example, Wimbledon makes all of their players wear outfits that are almost entirely white. This is considered a TRADITION of the competition, a bit like eating strawberries and cream when watching the games at Wimbledon.

PETRA MARTIĆ PLAYING AT WIMBLEDON

THE EQUIPMENT

RACKETS

Rackets are one of the most important pieces of tennis equipment you will need. It is important that your tennis racket has the right grip size and weight for how you play.

WHEN YOU GRIP A TENNIS RACKET, YOU SHOULD BE ABLE TO FIT YOUR FINGER IN THE GAP BETWEEN YOUR FINGERS AND THUMB.

BALLS

The ball is covered in FLUORESCENT yellow fabric that helps the ball to be seen. Every tennis ball is the same size as it is a standardised object in the sport. The ball must have a diameter of 6.54–6.86 centimetres (cm) and must weigh between 56 and 59.4 grams.

STANDARDISED OBJECTS MAKE SURE THAT THE GAME IS FAIR BY MAKING SURE EVERY GAME IS PLAYED WITH THE SAME TYPE OF EQUIPMENT EVERY TIME.

NETS

The net is stretched across the whole width of the court and splits the court into two halves. The net is 1.07 metres (m) high at either end and 0.91 m high in the centre. Other than for the serve, the ball is allowed to hit the net as long as it still goes over the net and on to your opponent's side.

TURN THE PAGE TO SEE HOW BIG THE COURT IS AND HOW IT IS LAID OUT.

HAWK-EYE

Since 2007, Grand Slams have been using Hawk-Eye technology. This technology is used in a number of professional sports games. The technology can track the ball and show where a ball landed and whether it was **in** or **out**. This technology helps tennis officials and umpires when it is not obvious whether a ball was in or out.

TURN TO PAGE 23 TO FIND OUT MORE ABOUT GRAND SLAMS.

CHASE   REVIEW

HAWK-EYE VIEW

OUT PLAYER CHALLENGE

THE COURT

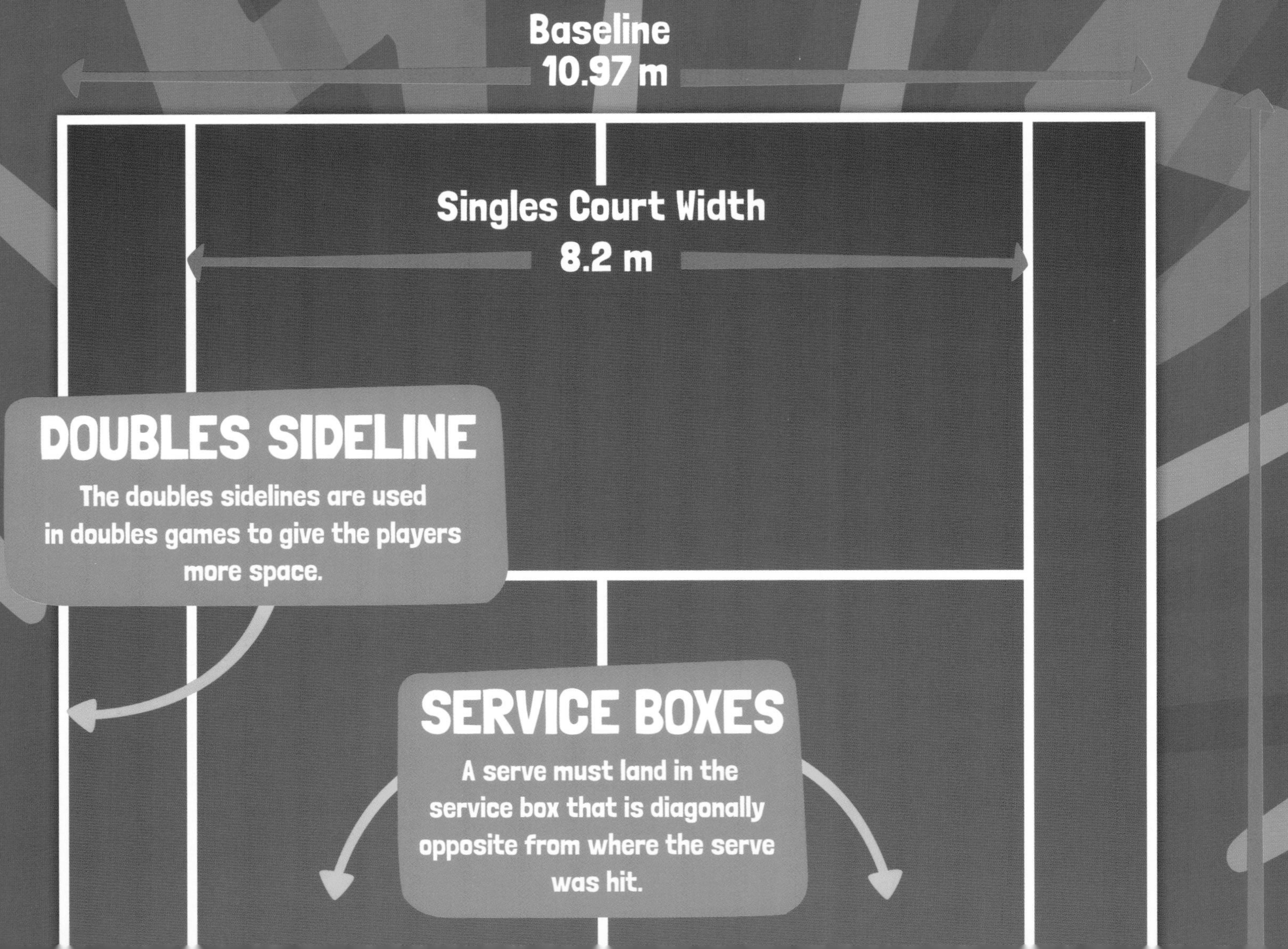

Baseline
10.97 m

Singles Court Width
8.2 m

DOUBLES SIDELINE

The doubles sidelines are used in doubles games to give the players more space.

SERVICE BOXES

A serve must land in the service box that is diagonally opposite from where the serve was hit.

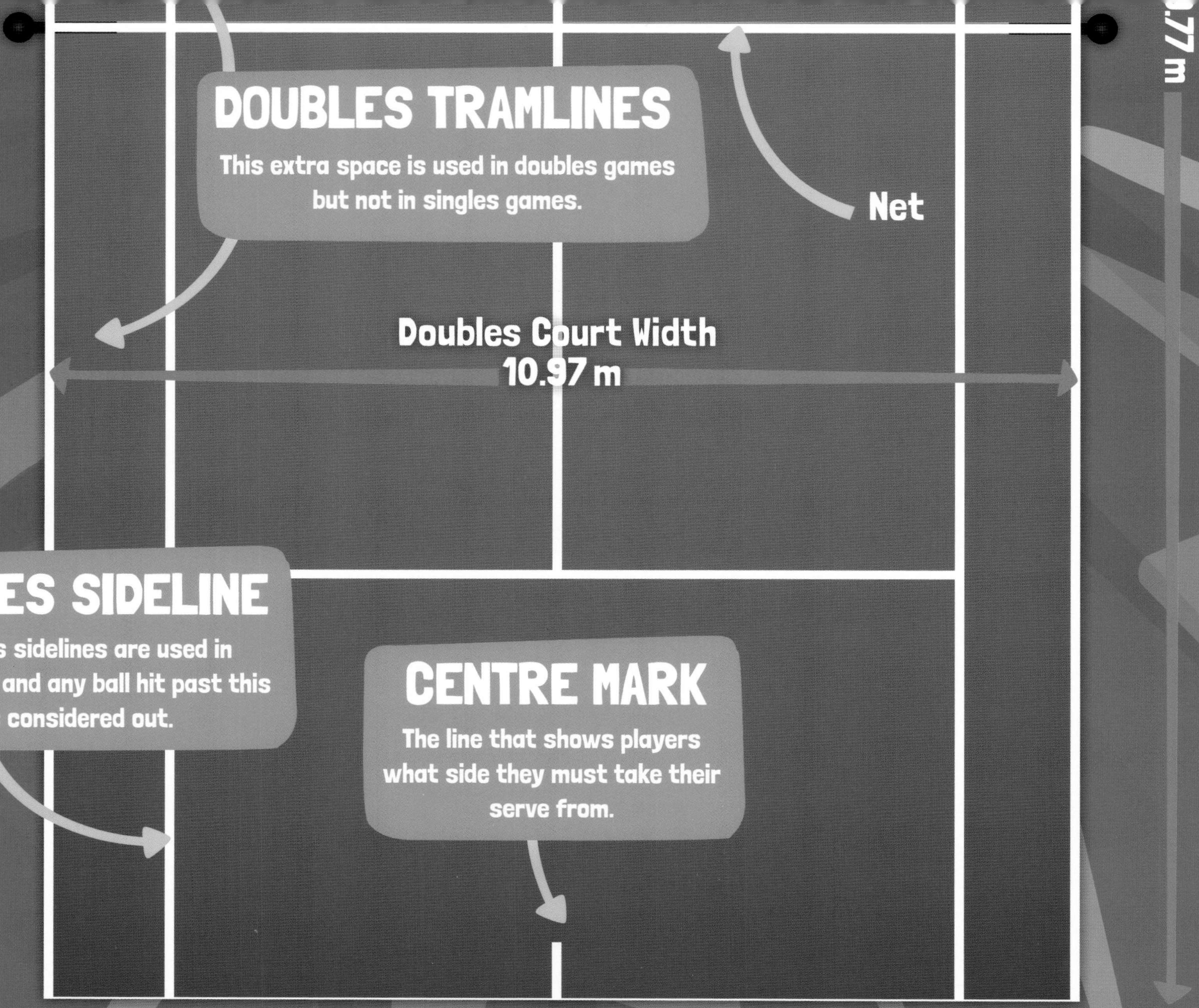

Net

DOUBLES TRAMLINES

This extra space is used in doubles games but not in singles games.

Doubles Court Width
10.97 m

CENTRE MARK

The line that shows players what side they must take their serve from.

SINGLES SIDELINE

The singles sidelines are used in singles games and any ball hit past this line is considered out.

THE RULES

SCORING

Tennis scoring is slightly different to other sports. You need to score a minimum of four points to win a game of tennis but they aren't called point 1, 2, 3 and 4. Instead they are called 15, 30, 40, and game point.

If two players are both on 40 then they go to deuce. The players will then need to score extra points to win that game. Whoever wins the next point gets an advantage, or 'A' for short. They then have to score the next point in order to win.

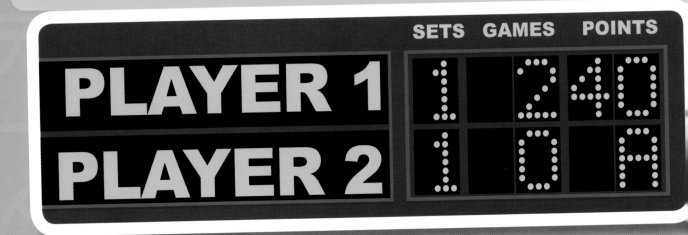

	SETS	GAMES	POINTS
PLAYER 1	1	2	40
PLAYER 2	1	0	A

To win a match of women's tennis, you have to win the best of three sets. To win a set, a player must be the first to win six games and be two games ahead of their opponent.

SVETLANA KUZNETSOVA LIFTING THE CITI OPEN TROPHY

GAINING POINTS

Gaining points is simple. You will gain a point if you hit the ball inside the boundaries and your opponent can't hit it back!

GIVING AWAY POINTS

Giving away points is more complicated. A point will be awarded to your opponent if:

- You have two serving <u>faults</u> in a row

- You don't return the ball before it bounces for a second time

- You return a ball but it goes outside the boundaries or hits the net without going over it and falls to the ground

- You touch the ball with your hand or body or more than once with your racket

- You touch the net when the ball is in play

- You hit the ball before it crosses over the net

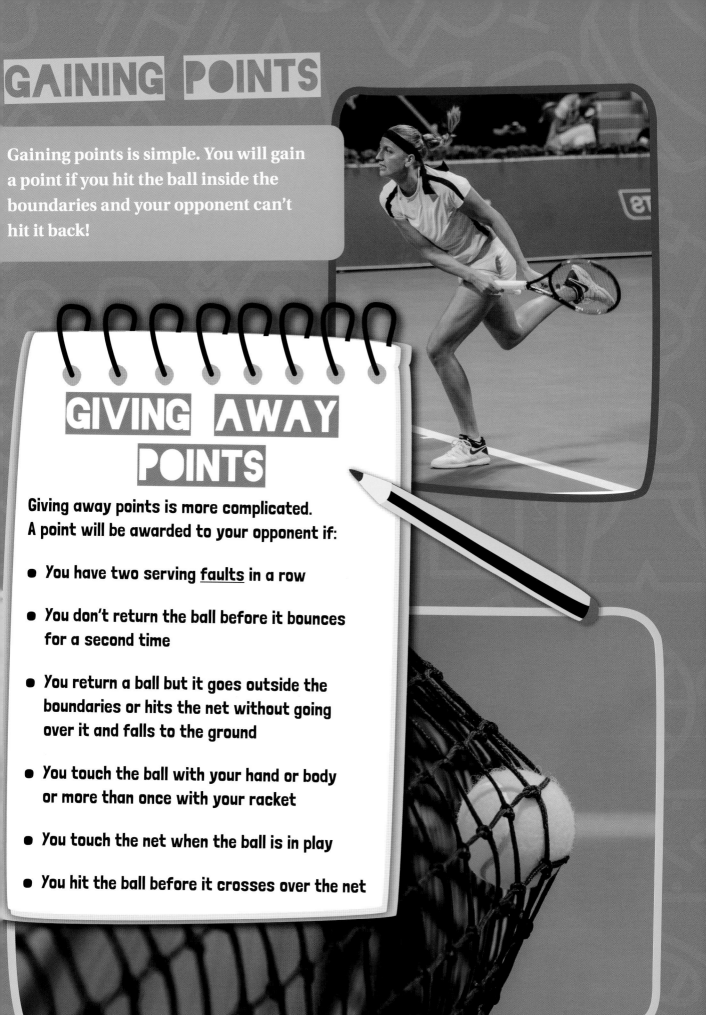

THE EVENTS

RECREATIONAL AND REGIONAL GAMES

If you play tennis at school, or play RECREATIONALLY, and you want to start competing in higher-level games, there are lots of ways you can get involved. Ask a teacher, parent or sports coach how to join your local tennis club.

CHILDREN PLAYING AT A TENNIS CLUB

THE BIG LEAGUES

As tennis players get better and better, they can start playing at higher levels. After regional games come national ones. This means you play people from all over your country. Then comes playing internationally, which means playing people from other countries.

PETRA KVITOVÁ, MONICA PUIG AND ANGELIQUE KERBER AT THE 2016 OLYMPIC GAMES

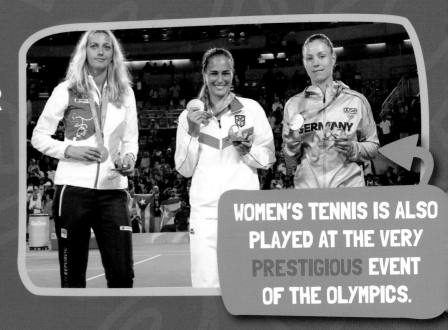

WOMEN'S TENNIS IS ALSO PLAYED AT THE VERY PRESTIGIOUS EVENT OF THE OLYMPICS.

WORLD TOURNAMENTS

WANG QIANG PLAYING IN THE THAILAND OPEN, 2015

In tennis, playing internationally means participating in world tournaments, which can be called either cups or opens. These tournaments happen all over the world. Cups usually have a set number of countries that can compete in them that are picked from QUALIFYING GAMES. Opens are where AMATEURS and professionals can play each other. Some of these include the China Open, the German Open and the Madrid Open.

GRAND SLAMS

There are four Grand Slams, or majors. These are the competitions that are considered the most prestigious tennis tournaments. They are the Australian Open, the French Open, the US Open and Wimbledon. Many professional tennis players want to win at least one Grand Slam title in their career, if not all four in the same SEASON.

WOMEN'S FINAL AT THE AUSTRALIAN OPEN, 2013

THE ONES TO WATCH

There are some very talented female tennis players out there right now. Let's find out some more about them.

SIMONA HALEP

FACT FILE:

Date of Birth:
27th September, 1991

Country of Birth:
Romania

Height:
1.68 m

Plays:
Right-Handed

Simona Halep managed to secure the Women's World Number 1 ranking in both 2017 and 2018. In 2018, she was awarded the WTA's Player of the Year Award and rightly so. Since turning professional in 2006, Halep's game has only grown stronger.

BELINDA BENCIC

FACT FILE:

Date of Birth:
10th March, 1997

Country of Birth:
Switzerland

Height:
1.75 m

Plays:
Right-Handed

Ranked as the Swiss Women's Number 1 tennis player in 2018, Bencic rose high up the rankings that year. This was all down to some key wins over players such as Venus Williams and Caroline Garcia.

PLAY LIKE A GIRL

GARBIÑE MUGURUZA

FACT FILE:

Date of Birth:
8th October, 1993

Country of Birth:
Venezuela

Height:
1.82 m

Plays:
Right-Handed

In 2017, Muguruza won her second Grand Slam title, beating Venus Williams in the Wimbledon final. After having beaten Serena Williams in the final of the 2016 French Open, Muguruza became the first woman to have defeated both Williams sisters in Grand Slam finals.

MADISON KEYS

FACT FILE:

Date of Birth:
17th February, 1995

Country of Birth:
USA

Height:
1.78 m

Plays:
Right-Handed

Since turning professional in 2009, Keys has made quite a name for herself, being known as having some of the most powerful serves and forehands in the game. She managed to hit the top 10 rankings in the world at the age of just 17 and went on to reach the Australian Open finals as a teenager as well.

THE HALL

There is a great history of female tennis players. Let's take a look at the best of the best.

Steffi Graf was one of the best tennis players of her time. With 22 Grand Slam titles to her name and some rather impressive ACCOLADES, she more than deserves a place in the hall of fame. She is the only person to have achieved the Golden Slam by winning all four Grand Slams and an Olympic Gold in the same year. She is also the only tennis player to have won each Grand Slam at least four times!

With a truly impressive number of Grand Slam titles to her name, Serena Williams has more than earned her place in the hall of fame, and she hasn't even RETIRED yet! She has won 23 Grand Slam singles titles and 14 doubles Grand Slams with her sister Venus. She is known for the power and strength she brings to the game.

OF FAME

Many people consider Margaret Court to be one of the best female tennis players of all time. She revolutionised women's tennis training and was one of the first women to include weight and cardio training into her routine. This gave her a great physical advantage on the court. To this day she holds the record for winning the most Grand Slam singles titles, with a total of 24.

Martina Navratilova is one of the most DECORATED tennis players of all time, particularly in doubles matches. She won an amazing 31 Grand Slam women's doubles titles and 10 Grand Slam mixed doubles. She also holds the record for most Wimbledon singles titles, having won it an astonishing nine times!

THE FACTS AND STATS

SETS	GAMES	POINTS
1	2	0
1	0	15

INSTEAD OF SAYING A PLAYER HAS ZERO POINTS, IT WILL OFTEN BE SAID AS 'LOVE'. FOR EXAMPLE: 'LOVE–FIFTEEN'.

IN THE LATE 1800S, WOMEN USED TO PLAY TENNIS IN FULL DRESSES!

IF A BALL HITS A PLAYER'S BODY OR ANY PART OF THEIR CLOTHING, THE POINT IS AWARDED TO THEIR OPPONENT, EVEN IF THE BALL WAS GOING OUT ANYWAY!

THE FASTEST SERVE EVER RECORDED BY A FEMALE TENNIS PLAYER WAS HIT BY SABINE LISICKI WHO SMASHED THE BALL AT OVER 210 KILOMETRES PER HOUR!

THIS IS RUFUS; HE IS A HAWK WHOSE JOB IT IS TO KEEP WIMBLEDON'S COURTS FREE OF PIGEONS!

ESTHER VERGEER, A WHEELCHAIR TENNIS CHAMPION, WON AN IMPRESSIVE 470 MATCHES IN A ROW AND PLAYED FOR 10 YEARS UNBEATEN UNTIL HER RETIREMENT IN 2013.

YOUR TRAINING

If tennis sounds like the sport for you, why not start practising and training? Ask your friends and see if they want to give it a go. Go to your local tennis courts or maybe even join a club.

Remember to practise all the different skills as much as you can! You never know – if you enjoy it, and you keep training, you might be in the hall of fame one day!

GLOSSARY

accolades — marks of approval or awards

amateurs — people who do something for fun rather than professionally

boundaries — the edges or limits of something

breathable — something that lets air pass through it

cardiovascular system — a system in the body that circulates blood around the body

concedes — gives up or gives in

decorated — in a profession, this is when you have been given awards, medals or trophies for your work

dominant — most important or strongest

fluorescent — very brightly coloured

manoeuvre — to move around

prestigious — having an important and highly-regarded status

professional — doing something you are good at as work

qualifying games — matches that a player must go through in order to compete in certain competitions, often cup tournaments

recreationally — to do something for fun rather than professionally

retired — to have stopped working professionally

season — a period of one year in which professional sports games take place

tactically — to work using a plan that will help you achieve certain goals

tradition — a behaviour or belief that is part of a long-established custom

WTA — Women's Tennis Association; the organisation that governs and promotes women's tennis worldwide

INDEX